Hundreds of Travel Hacks and Tips

260 to be exact.

By Bobby Boomer

Copyright 2018

Thank you for downloading this book. You now have what I believe is the most comprehensive list of travel hacks and tips assembled in one book.

This book was written for primarily a senior citizen reader however, most of these tips apply to many travelers.

Some items on the list will be familiar to you. Some will be <u>very</u> obvious, like remembering to bring a backup pair of glasses. However, based on seeing reading glasses being sold in every airport and hotel gift shop, I'm sure many people forget to bring them. So, it's on the list.

I'm confident everybody will find something new. I've traveled extensively and I certainly learned a few things.

Some books list a tip in just a short sentence. Where appropriate, I've tried to add a brief explanation or comments to the tip so you'll understand the importance of the tip. I've also tried to add a photo if it helps to clarify things.

Although there's lots of good advice here, nobody can force you to adhere to any of my suggestions. Some of the items on this list I've known about for years but still don't do myself. We all do what we're comfortable doing when we travel. That's OK. However, read the list and think about how each suggestion might apply to you. If it makes sense, then adopt it.

Some of the tips here would be considered unethical. Frankly, I've listed some things I just won't do myself because I don't think they're ethical. However, I've listed them anyway so you can make up your own mind

I've placed hashtags (#) at the end of each tip. This is for searching if you are reading the electronic version. If you just want tips on cruises, for example, do a document search on #cruise.

If I save you some heartache while traveling, I'm glad I was able to help.

Enjoy!

About the Author

Bobby Boomer has traveled the world his whole life. He's visited almost sixty countries and adds to that total each year. He has been to five continents and has flown over two and a half million miles on airplanes. He also has been on over twenty cruise ships, both ocean and river.

After retiring from the software business, he started a manufacturing business in his garage and built it up to over nineteen million dollars in yearly revenues in seven years. He sold that business and has retired a second time. He now enjoys spending time with family and grandkids, golf, travelling, volunteering at an NGO that serves Haiti and Tanzania and, sharing his travel tips with others.

Hundreds of Travel Hacks and Tips

260 to be exact.

1. Have travel insurance

I have to admit, I've never been high on insurance or extended warranties. I did have term life insurance when I was younger and of course, automobile insurance and homeowner insurance. But that is about it. When buying a car or appliance I would quickly say, "no thanks, not interested" before the salesperson could even get one sentence in about extended warranties. But that has changed now that I'm older – at least as far as travel insurance goes.

As my body reminds me every time I get out of a chair or bed, I'm more fragile than when I was in my twenties. There is a very good chance most senior travelers have a pre-existing condition. We may rely on Medicare, which does not cover expenses outside the U.S.A (there are a few exceptions). We twist ankles, lose our balance, bump our bodies into things and generally are not as nimble as when we were younger. A vacation can turn into a disaster if we have a medical issue.

If you're an infrequent traveler, look into trip insurance. If you're like my wife and I and travel multiple times a year, an annual trip insurance policy may be for you. I have a policy with TravelGuard (I'm not affiliated, compensated or sponsored by TravelGuard) but you'll see there are many choices. Our annual premium is around $900 and it's a comprehensive policy including a medevac home if the condition warrants.

I have a friend that broke her leg in Israel a couple years ago. Her travel insurance came to her rescue and flew her home in First Class because no coach seats were available.

Be sure to read the fine print. Also, research the policies and company online. You'll find many horror stories of insurance companies denying benefits for various reasons. Be smart and make sure you understand exactly what is covered and what you must do to get travel benefits.

My wife and I are less worried now when we travel. I urge you to look into travel insurance.

Even if you're not a senior citizen, you should consider travel insurance. Things happen. Trips need to be canceled. People get sick or fall. I believe it's a good choice. #general #senior #flying #cruise

2. Carry duplicate prescriptions

Have doctor write out a generic name as many countries do not recognize our brand names. Find out the generic name in the language of the country you are visiting.

If you're like me, you put your prescription meds in a daily container reminder box. Mine has seven little boxes for each day of the week. I admit this is not the smartest way for me to travel to foreign countries. It is possible customs or law enforcement may ask for proof on the items in the bins. Or, you may lose it and need a replacement. Some prescriptions carry a different name in other countries. Lipitor, for example, may be called Stator, Atorvastatin Teva, Litorva, Torid, Atoris, Atorlip, Mactor, Lipvas, Sortis, Torvast, Torvacard, Totalip, and Tulip. Be sure you are able to get refills in the country you're visiting.

Use your phone to take pictures of your prescription bottles. #general #senior #cruise

3. Carry duplicate glasses.

I could get by without my long distance glasses because my eyesight is 20/30. However, I could not get by for long without reading glasses. I always have one or two cheapies in my carry-on bag. Reading glasses are always sold in airport shops so many people must not have brought a backup pair. #general #senior #flying #cruise

4. If you're a senior, you've earned the discount

Most hotels, rental cars, and airlines give discounts to seniors. Remember though, this may not be the lowest rate. Always check when booking reservations and tickets. Always ask the front desk clerk when checking into your hotel. Ask for discounts everywhere! Buses, trains, subways, museums, tours, restaurants, movies etc. all may give discounts. In Europe, they may be called concessions or pensioner's rate. Also, look up discount partners at AAA and AARP. Or better yet, download their apps on your phone or tablet. #general #senior #flying #cruise

5. Bring along sleeping pills

Thankfully, I don't need sleeping pills when at home. However, when I'm in a much different time zone, I want one to help me go to sleep when my body is saying it's time to get up. I've never had an issue getting a doctor to prescribe a small amount for me. When traveling East to Europe, I try to sleep on the plane although I rarely am successful. When traveling West to the U.S.A. or Asia/Pacific, I try to stay awake. When I arrive home in

California, it's usually evening and since I've been awake for 20-25 hours, I fall asleep quickly. #general #senior #flying #cruise

6. Keep a bag semi-packed at home

We all have items we only use when traveling. Things like travel toothbrush case, international converters, When storing luggage away, keep toiletries, toothbrush, important numbers (frequent flyer, credit cards, etc.) in the bag. You don't have to keep it 100% packed, just the small items you know you'll want to take next time. I store my luggage in the garage. In one bag, I keep some items that I'll want to take on my next trip. #general #senior #luggage #flying

7. For emergencies, ask for a compassion discount

Although it used to be easier to get a compassion fare discount, some still offer it. It doesn't hurt to ask the airline, rental car, and hotels if they have a compassion fare or discount. #general #hotels #flying #cars #cruise

8. Put something in the room safe you can't forget

Although I've never forgotten to empty out the safe in my room, I've come close a few times. Here's a trick: Put one of the shoes you plan to wear that day in the safe. It's hard to check out of the hotel wearing just one shoe! Or perhaps your reading glasses or belt. #hotel #cruise

9. Bring snacks and water aboard your flight

The days of getting a warm meal – or any meal – on a domestic flight are gone. You'll get one on a long International flight but if you're flying in coach, that's about the only time. Thankfully, airport restaurants have upgraded offerings and they are ready to make your order 'to go.' If you plan a layover in a large airport, check the airport's website for information on restaurants available. Or, go to http://www.eater.com/airport-dining-guides for info on some of the larger airports in the U.S.A. A three-hour flight might turn into a five-hour flight and you'll be glad you have something to snack. #flying #general

10. Travel in shoulder seasons, not prime seasons

Fares go up on planes, hotels, cruise ships and other popular destinations during the busy times of the year. Airfares drop dramatically in September. Think about delaying your trip to a time that is not so busy before you buy those tickets. #flying #hotel #cruise #general

11. Pack light

Food is very different in other parts of the For decades I would come home from a trip with clothes in my suitcase that I never wore. No more. Who cares if somebody on a cruise sees you in a shirt on day five that you also wore on day one? I don't. I use the ship laundry frequently. #flying #hotel #cruise

12. Check your bag is you think it will be an issue

I am a dedicated carry-on person. However, I will check a bag if I think it will be an issue for me during a connection or helping a member of my party with their bags. #flying #luggage

13. Check connecting times carefully before booking

Plane travel is stressful. Don't make it worse by having a tight connection. Many times, you could have booked a flight leaving an hour or so earlier or later for the same fare. #flying

14. Check review sites and Google maps before booking hotels

Over a decade ago, before Google maps, I booked a nice hotel in Paris. It was off the beaten path and had great prices. The hotel only had a closely cropped picture of the front of the hotel. Upon arriving, I realized it was in the middle of a red light district and there was a sex shop right next door. Checking may also show you the hotel is isolated, or on a hill, or some other reason you might want to stay somewhere else. #hotel

15. Consider ground floor rooms in Europe

Some hotels in Europe only have stairs. However, a ground floor room could be a security issue so consider that when booking. #hotel

16. Never put "maid service please" on the door handle

Burglars look for these door hangers when walking through hallways at hotels. #hotel

17. Always put the security lock on when in room

Seems like common sense but surprisingly, most victims of hotel burglaries admit they did not have it locked while in their room. #hotel

18. Ask for a room near the elevator when making a reservation

More foot traffic but it will deter the burglars that look for rooms away from lots of foot traffic. #hotel

19. Watch what you eat!

Food is very different in other parts of the world. I sometimes carry an antibiotic if I expect I may get an intestinal disorder. #Dining #hotel

20. Don't leave meds lying in the open in your hotel room

A chatty housekeeper once told me if she was a druggy, she could make good money by daily stealing one or two opioids, sleeping pills, etc., from bottles left on counters. #hotel

21. Leave the expensive bling at home

You're traveling. You don't need that jewelry and bling. #general

22. Rent a phone when you land

Many smart travelers simply rent a burner (throw-away) phone when they land in a foreign country. Probably not worth it for a short visit but it could be cheaper than an international plan from your cell provider. This works especially well when there are large parties of travelers. Buy two or three phones and spread around as the group may separate. #general

23. Comfortable shoes - always!

Who cares about style – we're old enough to get away with our quirks! You see more and more people with business attire and tennis shoes. I love this trend! #general

24. Check with AARP.com and AAA.com

Not paid to say this but you can get some good discounts there. Check once a month. #general

25. Carry an empty lip balm case with two $100 bills rolled up inside

I will probably have to smash it to get them out but they're there in my backpack for an emergency. #general

26. Save money by shopping at grocery stores in a strange city

Yes, convenience stores are more convenient but also more expensive. When we go to Honolulu, our first stop after the airport is the Costco near town. We buy food, t-shirts, rafts, hats, etc. #general

27. Buses vs. taxis

Instead of an expensive taxi, try a bus. Much cheaper and we enjoyed people watching and at times, chatting with the locals. One of our memorable rides was a bus from the cruise terminal in Puerto Vallarta to downtown. We still laugh about it. #general

28. Put a dryer sheet in your luggage

Want your clothes to smell fresher after they've been in luggage for a day? Try this hack. #luggage

29. Consider compression stockings for long flights

30. Carry your doctor's phone number

Also, get his/her email. In an emergency, you'll be glad to have them. #general

31. Flight attendants are a great resource for tips on shopping, eating, etc.

Flying to a new international city? Try to start a conversation with a flight attendant if they're not busy and seem interested in helping you. They know the city well and can recommend restaurants, shopping, etc. I once spent almost an hour talking to an FA on a long flight to Shanghai. She was a huge source of information. #flying

32. Exercise in flight

DVT (Deep Vein Thrombosis) is real and it can kill you. Get out of your seat and move every 90 minutes or so. However, don't be the annoying passenger that does gym exercises in the aisles. Just stretch and bit and move your legs. #flying #senior

33. Booze and caffeine

I admit I have self-medicated myself many times while flying long-haul flights. As I got older, I realized it was not helping me with jet lag and anxiety on the flight. Now, I drink a glass of wine (ok – maybe two) then switch to water. #flying #senior

34. Jet lag becomes harder as we get older

On a recent European cruise, we arrived four days early so we could get adjusted to the new time zone. If possible, get to your destination a day or two early if you need to be sharp on a certain day. #flying #cruise

35. How to wash clothes in a hotel sink

If you need to wash clothes in the hotel sink, use the body wash instead of soaps and shampoos. Body wash is gentler than other soaps offered free at hotels. #hotel

36. Carry a dummy wallet

Let the thieves take a wallet that is empty of anything valuable. #general

37. Always know where the U.S. embassy is in every city you're visiting

Put their phone number and address on your phone. You never know when you might need it. #general

38. Want to turn your cell phone into a louder speaker?

Put it inside a coffee cup. This will make the volume higher. #general

39. Carry a small packet of baby wipes in your carry-on bag

You'll use them more than you think. I wear a Panama hat and it gets sweaty. The wipes are perfect for removing the sweat. #general

40. How to get a phone or computer charger from a hotel

If you left your phone or computer charger at home, ask the hotel front desk. They usually have dozens in storage that have been left by other guests. A clerk once took me into the lost and found room and I was told the dozens of chargers were there from just the past month. They take them to a charity once a month. #hotel

41. Call the local embassy if you get ill

They can recommend doctors, hospitals, and pharmacies. #general

42. Don't know the password at a restaurant, hotel, bar, etc.?

Use your phone to check FourSquare.com for passwords. #general

43. Carry a medical alert card

You may not have serious ailments but you need to let emergency personnel know quickly what medicines you are taking and any issues you have. Always carry this information in your wallet or purse. #general

44. Immunizations

Check with the U.S. State dept. for advisories on travel to various countries. Better yet, check http://wwwnc.cdc.gov/travel/#general

45. Water, water, water

Drink lots of water while flying and traveling. I can't emphasize this enough. #general

46. Daily deal sites like Groupon and Living Social and mail offers

I know a lot about deals on Groupon and Living Social. I owned a printing company that sold over 100,000 deals. Yes, you can get good deals but....If it seems too good, it probably is. These deals have lots of fine print. Flyers received in the mail have lots of fine print. Make sure you will be happy with the offer. The $1000 deal for seven days in Italy including airfare may include a charter plane with tiny seats and hotel you might not be comfortable staying. #general

47. Veterans Administration medical does not cover medical issues outside the U.S.A.

See number one above. #general

48. Enroll in Smart Traveler Enrollment Program (STEP) at https://step.state.gov/step/

You'll receive important info from Embassies about safety in countries, help with contacting embassies and family and friends can reach you easier. #general

49. Carry antiseptic wipes.

Wipe everything in the room that is touched frequently. Start with the remote control, then light switches, doors, handles, etc. #hotel, #Flying

50. Wash the hotel drinking glasses

It's been reported many times: Hotel housekeepers sometimes skip washing the glasses and will just wipe them with a dirty cleaning rag. Some maids do not clean them at all. They're in a hurry and under pressure to finish their allotted rooms. Don't drink from them until you wash them. #hotel

51. Do your research!

Don't leave your vacation to chance. Read the fine print. Use the Internet. Check review sites such as tripadvisor.com. Do an Internet search on that hotel, cruise, destination spot, etc. #general

52. Worried about getting your camera wet in inclement weather?

Use the free shower cap from the hotel room to protect the camera. #hotel #general

53. Don't rent a cart

Want to save $3 for a rental cart at the airport? Walk outside and look near the curb or taxi area. #airport

54. Always put your flight info on rental car reservation

Sometimes at smaller airports, they close and go home if they don't know your flight number. More than once I've walked up to a rental counter late at night and was greeted by name. They were waiting for me. #cars

55. Don't pay $4 for a bottle of water

Bring an empty bottle or thermos from home and fill up once past security. Most airports have refill stations now. Also, bring a Gatorade packet or other type of flavoring. #airports

56. The day most airlines lower their prices

Most airlines have price adjustments on Tuesday afternoons. They can happen anytime but historically, the majority of them happen on Tuesdays. #flying

57. If a flight is canceled, call reservation number while waiting in line.

Let's say you're at the gate. An announcement is made that the flight has been canceled. You are asked to get in line. Do that but while you're walking, call the airlines central reservation number. Chances are you'll get your flight resolved before you reach the gate counter. If you like what the reservation rep did on the phone, get out of line. If you're not happy, stay in line and be nice to the counter rep. Maybe they can do something better for you. #flying

58. Check www.seatguru.com before booking any seat

Enter your airlines and flight number and you'll see detailed info on every seat on your plane. #flying

59. Worried about liquids coming out of caps that are not tightly sealed?

Put some kitchen wrap (Saran Wrap, Plastic Wrap) under the cap before tightening. #general

60. Want the whole can of soda pop?

Flight attendants are usually happy to give you a full can of your drink. Just ask. #flying

61. Be ready for TSA BEFORE you get there

Take off your belt. Put all money and trash from your pocket in a ziplock bag. #flying

62. When packing clothes, roll them up instead of folding

Saves space and I have found they don't wrinkle as much as when folded. #general

63. Use dry cleaning bags to keep out wrinkles

I always put my shirts and slacks inside a dry cleaning plastic bag. Not sure why but it really reduces wrinkles. #luggage

64. Honey will get you so much farther than vinegar with customer service reps

If really angry, take a breath and slow down. I once was on a three-week cruise. There was a drummer in a band right above our ceiling. I know because I went up and checked. The front desk lady said there was no live music playing and I should turn down my radio! This went on for a few minutes until she hung up on me! I was ready to scream! I thought of charging down to the front desk but I decided to wait until the next morning to discuss with a supervisor. By that time, I was calm and speaking logically. I spoke to the hotel director and she said I should go to my room and she would be there soon to take me to my new room. She arrived quickly and escorted me to an Owner's Suite! Honey vs vinegar. #general

65. Stop at the newsstand before security and ask for a large shopping bag

Put all your stuff in there like coins, money, wallet, keys, etc. Put it inside your carry-on bag or, just make it a second carry-on bag to the gate agents. #general

66. Want a quiet place to rest while on a long layover at the airport?

Find the chapel and go rest there. However, do NOT be noisy and talk on cell phones. #flying

67. Pack an extension strip in your carry-on bag.

Mine is just three feet long. You'll use it at the airport, hotel room, aircraft, cruise ship cabin. Plus, you'll make friends at the airport that will want to plugin to your strip. Your neighbors at the airport will love you. #general

68. The Wi-Fi password for Delta is usually "thankyou"

It hasn't changed in years but may be changed by the time you read this. If you're near one of their lounges or crew lounge, try it out. #general

69. How to save on overweight bag fees

If your bag is overweight, the fee from the airlines may be very high. It may be cheaper to buy a cheap bag at the airport gift shop and check it. #luggage

70. How diabetics avoid having to check a bag at the gate

Airlines cannot force you to check a bag if you're a diabetic and have insulin in the bag. #luggage #flying

71. Don't get out of your seat.

Duplicate seating doesn't happen much anymore. However, if somebody approaches you and says you're in their seat, check your boarding pass. If you both have the same seat, do NOT get up. You were there first and it's your seat. The other person will be reassigned a new seat which may be a middle seat. In some cases, they'll get a first class seat then you'll wish you never read this tip! #flying

72. If you travel more than once or twice a year internationally, get a GOES card

It will save time clearing customs. #general

73. The shorter the layover, the higher a chance for a luggage issue

Short layovers at a connecting city significantly increase the chances of your luggage not making the connections. Try to have at least 90 minutes between flights if you plan to check bags.

74. Untie your shoes while waiting to get through TSA at airport

Going through the TSA inspection can be stressful. Be prepared. #flying

75. Can't find a power outlet at the airport?

Ask the airport personnel where the wall outlets are located. They probably know of few that are hidden. #flying

76. Don't buy black luggage

If you have black luggage, put a ribbon or something to make it stand out on the luggage carousel. #flying

77. Tags on bags fall off

The less you have hanging from your bag, the better. Name tag straps will probably come off at some point. Name tags taped to the bag will be there much longer. I personally tape a business card to all my bags. Also, put identification inside the bag.

78. How to charge phone fast at the airport

If you have a low battery on your phone and only a few minutes to charge, put your phone in airplane mode first. It will charge faster. However, you won't be able to text or make/receive calls. #flying

79. Medical equipment in bags gets checked for free

If you're carrying medical equipment in a bag, you don't have to pay baggage fees. #flying

80. Lost and Found at airports

Airports have multiple lost and found rooms. Don't just go to one if there is a chance it could be at others. Airlines, security, cleaning crew, etc. all have lost and found. #flying

81. If you're not in a rush to get to your destination, volunteer for the bumps

You'll get compensation and maybe a first class seat on the next plane. #flying

82. Copy of passport

An easy way to get a copy is to just take a photo of them with your phone or tablet. #general

83. Use Duty-Free to avoid baggage charges

If you're on an International flight and your bag is over the weight limit, buy something from duty free and put your overweight stuff in the duty-free bag. The airlines have to let you board with the duty-free bag. #flying

84. Don't put vibrating items in checked bags.

If you put something with batteries that vibrates like an electric toothbrush in your checked bag and it starts to vibrate, you'll need to open the bag and turn it off. Ramp agents will take you off the plane, open your bag and have you turn it off. #flying

85. Extra charging ports hidden in hotel rooms

Most TVs in hotel rooms now have a USB port. This means you can charge your phone or tablet from the hotel TV. #hotel

86. Taking food through TSA security

Many believe you can't take food through security. You can as long as the liquids, i.e. soups, gravies, etc., don't contain more than 3.4 ounces. You don't need to buy your meal at the airport once you clear security. Bring it from home or stop along the way to the airport. #flying

87. Why you should avoid late night flights

Last flights of the day that get canceled for weather issues will mean you spend the night at the airport or at a hotel, at your own expense. #flying

88. What to do with a dead phone at the airport

When you're at the airport and you have a dead cell phone and need to make a call, pick up any phone at an empty counter and dial 9 for an outside line. This doesn't always work but does most times. #flying

89. Use Twitter if you've been mistreated

If you've been mistreated by an airline, rental car, cruise line or hotel, put your comments on Twitter and copy the respective Twitter account for the offending business. I've done this a few times and I received immediate attention. #general

90. Strong odors on planes

Use deodorant and go light on the perfumes and colognes. Your fellow passengers will appreciate you doing that. #flying

91. Hotel shower caps and dirty shoes

Have dirty shoes that need to be packed in luggage? Put a shower cap around them. Many hotel rooms have free shower caps. #hotel #luggage

92. What to do when airline damages your luggage

If your bag gets damaged, file a complaint with the airline that damaged it. They'll fix it or replace it. Most people think airlines only compensate for lost luggage. #flying #luggage

93. Gate agents have the power to upgrade you.

Flight attendants usually do not have the power to upgrade you while the door is open. #flying

94. This trick may get you an upgrade to first class

Bring small gifts for flight attendants. Food, candy, lapel pins, etc. I have given out lapel pins that show an angel sitting on an airplane wing to hundreds of flight crews and gate agents. I do this because I want to do it.

However, I have been given upgrades, free booze and even bottles of wine to take home. #flying

95. How to get into an airline club without a membership

Want to get into an airline lounge but don't belong to the club? Stand outside the door and wait for somebody entering. Say, "Excuse me. I have an unexpectedly long layover. Would you mind guest-ing me into the lounge?" You won't have to ask many before you're inside the lounge. If the drinks are not free, buy your host a drink. #flying

96. How to avoid long check-in lines at the airport

Check-in for flights online at home. Avoid the long check-in lines for those without boarding passes. Check your bags with the outside agent then walk straight to your gate. #flying

97. How to keep earbuds and chargers safe

Earbuds and chargers always loose in your purse or travel bag? Put them in an old eyeglass case. #general

98. How to legally take liquids through TSA screening

Parents traveling with infants are allowed to bring liquids through security. #flying

99. How to avoid middle seat when the plane is full

When checking in online and only middle seats are available, don't accept one. Don't check-in. When you get to the airport, you may still get a middle seat but you have a good chance of getting an upgrade to the bigger seats including first class. #flying

100. Do this before unpacking in your hotel room

Check your room thoroughly before unpacking. It will be easier to change rooms this way should you find the room unacceptable. #hotel

101. Check bedding at hotel thoroughly

Bedspreads and blankets are cleaned infrequently at hotels. Even if the hotels claim they do clean them for each guest, don't rely on it. #hotel

102. How to cancel a hotel reservation past the deadline

If you need to cancel your hotel reservation and it's past the cancellation deadline, change the reservation to a later date that is within the cancellation period. Then, call back 12 hours later and speak to somebody else. You'll be able to cancel without a fee. #hotel

103. How to get a great hotel room rate

To get a good rate for a hotel room, call the hotel directly and speak to the manager on duty or sales manager. Do not let them transfer you to a central reservation office. Ask for a good rate. Negotiate. Persuade. You can get a rate much lower than what is offered on their website. #hotel

104. You probably don't know this about third-party booking sites

Know this: Expedia, Priceline, Hotels dot com, Hotwire, Orbitz, Trivago, CheapTickets, ebookers and others are all owned by Expedia or Priceline. #general

105. Smoking tip for non-smoking hotel rooms

If you smoke in a non-smoking room at a hotel, you will get charged even after check-out. Your odds of getting away with it are slim. #hotel

106. Ice bucket tip for hotel rooms

Never use the ice bucket in a hotel room or cruise ship cabin without using the liner. Just saying. #hotel

107. Don't buy a toothbrush or a razor if you forget them at home

Many hotels have free stuff at the front desk such as toothbrushes, toothpaste, razors, etc. #hotel

108. How to beat prices on third-party booking sites

Check hotels rates at the online booking sites (i.e. Expedia, Orbitz, Trivago, etc.) then call the hotel and ask if they can beat the rate. Usually, they'll be happy to do that since they'll make more money than if they paid a fee to the online booking site. Plus, you'll get reward benefits if applicable. #hotel

109. Housekeeping carts in aisles

Hotel maids do not like it when you are caught taking things off their cart. However, hotel maids are usually very happy to give you whatever you want from their cart. Need a dozen bars of soap? No problem. #hotel

110. How to avoid "based on double occupancy" rates

Single traveler and you don't want to pay the single fare on a cruise? Call them and ask them to waive or reduce the fee. If the cruise is not going to sell out, they may do it. It's a long shot but worth a shot. Or, check out the single cabins now offered on some cruise ships. #cruise

111. Extra security for phones, computers, etc.

Tape business card or label to phone, laptop, charger, tablet, etc. A good person may find it and contact you. I have my business card taped on everything. #general

112. Don't make this mistake when booking flights and hotels

These sites track your past visits. They may raise a price on a subsequent visit. Clear your cache and cookies when booking reservations online. #hotel #flights

113. When a double room can turn into a single room

It can happen on any hotel reservation. The fine print on hotel reservations says requests can't be guaranteed. Double beds may turn into a king or vice versa. The later in the day you check-in, the greater the odds of this happening. #hotel

114. Get the date right on International hotel bookings

This happens more than you might imagine. Let's say you take an overnight flight from the U.S.A. on say the 18th but you arrive on the 19th. You forget that and book your hotel at your destination for the 18th. #hotel

115. Avoid debit cards at hotels and rental cars

Always use a credit card at hotels and rental cars. Debit cards may require a deposit that is not refunded for up to two weeks later. Also, credit cards offer immediate refunds for disputed charges. #hotel #cars

116. Don't forget to add in resort fees

The actual rate may be higher than a competitor's rate once resort fees are added. Be careful to add-in the resort fee at hotels. #hotel

117. When an image isn't reality

Hotels are notorious for enhancing their images through computer software. With a wide angle camera lens, they can make the space between the bed and the desk look twice as wide as normal. Be sure to check other sites such as Tripadvisor.com, Google maps, etc. to learn more about the room, hotel, street, and neighborhood. #hotel

118. When do hotel rooms usually go down in price?

Booking a hotel room more than thirty days in advance is generally a bad thing. Rates on hotels tend to go down as you get closer to your arrival date. Not always – but usually. The exception to this rule would be smaller, boutique hotels and B&B's that may sell out. #hotel

119. Flashlight app on your phone

Be sure to download a flashlight app for your smartphone. You'll use it often while traveling. #general

120. Travel size items are your friend

Bring along the small, travel-size laundry detergents boxes for washing out underwear and socks in the sink. Target stores, Wal-Mart, and others have large travel items sections. #general

121. Don't buy cheap luggage

Buy good luggage. I'm not suggesting designer bags with fancy logos. I am suggesting you pay a few dollars extra for a well-made brand. Cheap luggage breaks quickly. Wheels fall off. Locks and zippers break. I get most of mine at Costco and they're well made at a reasonable price. Plus, they have an excellent return policy. #luggage

122. Take cold and flu pills even if you don't need them now

Pick up a small first aid kit with medicines to pack in your luggage. I once started coming down with a cold in Germany and it was almost laughable trying to find the right cold medicine since I don't speak or read German. From that point on, I always carried daytime and nighttime cold medicine. #general

123. Why you need to hide a gift card

Buy a Visa or Master Card Gift Card. Load it with a couple hundred bucks. DON'T put it in your wallet. Hide it somewhere. You'll be glad you have this if your wallet or purse is ever missing. #general

124. Take pictures of credit cards, driver's license, Passport, etc. and store in the cloud.

Store in the cloud and not just on your portable computer devices (although storing a copy on those devices is a good idea too) so you can access them from any Internet computer in the world. #general

125. Another hotel safe trick

I like simply putting one shoe in the safe so I don't forget but, you could use this trick too. Pack a long length of string or cord in your luggage. If you use the hotel room safe, run the string from the safe to your luggage. This way, you'll NEVER forget anything inside the safe. Hotels find stuff in safes almost daily. Don't be one that leaves stuff there. #hotel

126. How to handle rain

Pack a cheap, plastic rain parka in your luggage. It won't take up much space and it will save you from a downpour. #general

127. Cell phone cameras

These days, cell phone cameras are almost as good as stand-alone cameras from just a few years ago. Unless you're a really good photographer, just use your cell-phone camera or if you can afford it, buy a small, palm-sized camera. Your phone and these cameras take surprisingly good images. #general

128. Tipping overseas
Do an Internet search on tipping practices for the countries you'll be visiting. Many countries do not expect tips. In some countries, you may actually offend somebody by tipping. #general

129. Pack a couple of large plastic bags for your dirty clothes.
#general

130. How to handle Gypsies
In some countries around Europe, tourists are approached by thieves or gypsies. They surround you and distract you to steal things from your pockets or purse. They may shove a map in your face and ask directions while their colleagues are going through your pockets. They also are experts at working in teams and are particularly crafty on buses and subways. I was once surrounded by four or five gypsy women in a train station in Rome. They shoved a small baby in my face and I felt hands on my clothes. I started swinging and yelling. They yelled back with some choice words but they left me alone. #general

131. Men, never carry your wallet in your back pocket.
#general

132. Ladies, always wear your purse around your neck, not just over your shoulder.
#general

133. How to speak a foreign language when you don't know a word
Your smartphone probably has language interpretations software. It's in Google apps on my phone. Or, download an app. They work great. Just speak into the app using the phone microphone and the app converts it to the language of choice. #general

134. How to find a great local restaurant
Ask police officers for restaurant tips. If they're walking a beat, they know the area very well and can give you great advice. #general

135. Why you need to think about cross-dressing

OK. I wrote that headline to get your attention. I always put one set of clothing in my wife's bag and vice-versa when we are forced to check bags. If one is lost, at least you'll have a backup. #luggage

136. How to shrink a tourist map to 3 inches

Don't want to carry a map in your pocket? Take a picture of it with your camera phone. #general

137. How to tell a taxi driver where you want to go if you don't speak the language

If in a foreign country and you don't speak the language, take a picture of your hotel to show to taxi drivers. Also, it's a good idea to have a picture of your room number since keys don't show your room number. #hotel

138. How to handle crying babies on planes

I always pack my noise-canceling headset. Yes, it takes up a little room in my backpack but they've saved me so many times from a crying baby, talkative neighbor, etc. #flying

139. Don't take the tunnel

In Las Vegas, if you're traveling from airport to a strip hotel, be sure to tell the driver, "No Tunnel." Taking the tunnel adds about $5 to the fare. The tunnel is faster if you're going downtown. #general

140. Mail – don't check

If you just can't get everything inside a carry-on, consider shipping your luggage. It may even be cheaper than checking the bag. You'll travel with less stress, won't have to wait in baggage claim for your bags, as they'll be at your hotel when you arrive. Yes, there is a slight chance there could be a delay but statistics show, it's a lot less of a chance for delay than if you checked them with the airline. #luggage #flying

141. Call your bank before you leave home

Choose the credit cards you plan to use on your trip. Then, call the credit card company, or visit their website, and let them know when and where you'll be traveling. This will avoid having charged declined. #general

142. Get cash when you land

Airport currency exchange rates are the worst! Just go to an ATM and withdraw money in the local currency. Even with the ATM fee, it will be cheaper. #general

143. Black slacks

I always pack, or wear, a black pair of jeans. They can become dress pants in a pinch. #general

144. Rethink that hotel

Airbnb.com is getting great reviews. You can rent a room, a guest cottage, or a whole house for very reasonable prices. However, watch out for the additional fees such as cleaning fees. #hotel

145. Juice it up

I never leave home on a long trip without my spare battery charger. I use a Mophie that is about the size of a pack of cigarettes. However, there are many others too. When my phone or camera gets low on juice, I just plug it into the Mophie and charge it back up. #general

146. Shake it up

Don't be afraid to rearrange the hotel or cruise cabin furniture if it makes your room more useful. If I'm in a room for more than a few days and it's hard to see the TV from the chair, I'll move the chair between the beds. Of course, always put it back when checking out. #cruise #hotel

147. Key card safety on cruise ships

Pack a couple of lanyards to use for attaching your cruise card or hotel key. We always do this on cruises. The front desk or gift shops can punch the hole on the card. #cruise

148. Take binoculars

Pack small binoculars. They'll be very useful as you explore your destination. They're

great for cruising or visiting other cities.
#Cruise

149. Non-cancellable rates

Hotels frequently offer a discounted rate
although it's "non-cancellable." If you're just
one or two days away from your trip, consider
calling the hotel and changing your rate to a
'non-cancellable' rate. #hotel

150. National Parks lifetime pass

Seniors 62 or older, and residents of the
U.S.A. can get a lifetime pass for the National
Parks for just $80. The pass is good for the
entire vehicle too (up to four adults). If you
buy over the Internet, however there is a $10
processing fee added. #general

151. Don't put carry-on luggage over your seat

Put your carry-on luggage across the aisle,
not over your seat. Also, put the zippers
facing out. This way, you'll be able to keep
an eye on your luggage. #flying

152. Don't have hotel room cleaned

Don't have your hotel room cleaned. Unless you've really made a mess, it's not worth the risk to me. Leave the "Do Not Disturb" sign on the outside door during your entire stay. This will protect your valuables. Call for towels if/when you need them. #hotel

153. Register all guests in the room.

If one forgets a key and is not on the folio, the front desk will not be able to give them a key. One time my wife had to wait a couple hours for me to return because she could not get a key at the front desk. #hotel

154. Ignore the menu slipped under your hotel door

If a take-out menu is ever slipped under your hotel room door, do NOT order from it. It could be a scam just to get your credit card info. Ask the front desk for take-out recommendations. #hotel

155. Cell phones on cruise ships

Turn off your phone on cruise ships. Or at least, put it in airplane mode. You may incur roaming charges even if you don't make any calls. #cruise

156. Watch those characters in costume

Don't let costumed characters pose for a picture until you have firmly negotiated the fee. Also, watch your pockets. Some are thieves or work with a third-party that steals from you while you're distracted. #general

157. They can say no, but can't say yes

Peter Greenberg, a well-known travel expert, advises, "Never take a no from someone not empowered to give you a yes in the first place." I love this advice. #General

158. When to hang up and call back.

Don't like the answers you're getting from a call center for an airline, hotel, rental car, cruise lines, etc., just say thank you I'll call back. Then, hang up and call back. You'll be surprised how many times you'll get the answer you want just by talking to another person. #general

159. Check the deck

When booking a cabin on a cruise ship, check the deck plans carefully. You never want to be under the pool, pool deck, teen club, dance floor, bandstand, etc. #cruise

160. Close the drapes

Be careful about cabin privacy while pulling into ports. I know a person that left their blinds open while pulling into a port. She came out of the shower in her birthday suit only to see cabins from a ship anchoring across the pier. People were looking right into her cabin and one waved to her! #cruise

161. When are cruises cheap?

Cruises are usually discounted between Thanksgiving – Christmas. Also, check prices right after Easter – but before summer. #cruise

162. Shrinkage on river cruises

If you're considering a river cruise on the Danube river, be aware that water levels are at times low in the summer and delays or cancellations occur. Consider Spring for Danube cruising. #cruise

163. Last minute cruise fares

Cruises booked at the last minute are sometimes lower in price but may have the most undesirable cabin locations on the ship. #cruise

164. What to do on long layovers

Some airports have massage services, meditation rooms, and chapels. If you're stuck in an airport with a long layover, go online and look at a map of your terminal. #flying

165. Flight crews have authority

If an airline flight attendant gives you a direct command, consider he/she is wearing a peace officer's badge. If you don't follow his/her directions, they can have you arrested when the plane lands. #flying

166. How to travel with jewelry

Use a large weekly pill container for your jewelry when traveling. #general

167. Pack like a pro

Empty shoes in your luggage are perfect for stashing socks and underwear. #luggage

168. Keep the change

Don't bring home loose change from a foreign country. Give it to a homeless person or as a tip to someone as you're leaving. Banks will not take foreign coins #general

169. Adjoining aisle seats

My wife and I both like aisle seats. We sit across the aisle from each other. We are always surprised when people tell us they never thought about doing that. #flying

170. Call 111

911 is the emergency number in the U.S.A. In many other countries, it's 112. #general

171. Hotel business cards

Many hotels have a business card at the reception desk. Take one for showing taxi drivers exactly where you want to go. In many countries, taxi drivers do not speak English. #hotel

172. Get guaranteed TSA Pre-Check

Get TSA Pre-Check for five years by applying at U.S. Customs. It cost $85 and will get you TSA Pre for five years. If you travel a lot internationally, pay $100 and get Global Entry. It will speed you through customs lines when arriving back in the U.S.A. and also includes TSA Pre for five years. #general

173. Wear the winter coat on the plane

Wear your heavy, bulky things on the plane. Sure, you may look a little strange wearing that heavy winter coat through the airport when its 85 degrees outside but it won't take up valuable space in your bag. Once on the plane, take it off and store it above your seat. #flying

174. Leave your nice clothes home

I sometimes bring old, worn clothes on vacation. If I buy too much, I can leave the clothes in the hotel and put my purchases in my suitcase. #luggage

175. Free Wi-Fi at airports

At some airports, you can get an hour of free Wi-Fi___33. If you want more time for free, change the clock on your computer by rolling it back 50 or 55 minutes. Don't forget to change it back. #flying

176. Zip ties

Use zip ties to secure the zippers on your luggage. If TSA needs to open your bags, zips ties are much cheaper than the locks they break when they open your bags. #luggage

177. More free Wi-Fi

Airline clubs have free Wi-Fi and it's usually available even outside the club if you're nearby. Camp out near the club and get their free Wi-Fi. #flying

178. Play ball on the flight

On a long flight, put a golf or tennis ball under your foot for a soothing massage. Be careful not to let it roll away! #flying

179. When to fly

Sunday is usually the most expensive day to fly. Tuesday is usually the cheapest. #flying

180. How to pack collared shirts

To keep collars on shirts wrinkle-free, put your rolled-up belt inside the collar. #luggage

181. How to pack q-tips

Old, large prescription pill bottles are great for q-tips. #luggage

181. Have a sweater or scarf handy on planes.

Planes can get cold by doors. Those big, long chunky scarves are great to take on a plane. They'll keep you warm or double as a pillow. #flying

182. How to pack thin chains

Put those thin, necklace chains through a straw before packing. They'll never get tangled. #general

183. Where did I park my car?

Use your phone to take a picture of your car in the airport parking lot. Include in the picture a reference point such as a sign, building, tree, etc. #general

184. Fly farther away from home.

If you live in an area with multiple airports within 100 miles, check them all when requesting fare quotes. The extra hour drive to an outlying airport could save you lots of money. #flying

185. The greatest place to book a rental car is....

Costco Travel. You have to be a Costco member but their rates are always very good. #cars

186. The lowest airfare of the day usually is...

Generally speaking, flights departing after 8:00 PM each day are cheaper than those departing earlier in the day. #flying

187. The cheapest airfares are…

If you really want to save money and don't mind an overnight flight, check those redeye fares. You'll also save on a hotel room! #flying

188. Use this tip and frequent flyer miles will NEVER expire

Don't let frequent flyer miles expire. Even if you don't plan to fly, you can extend the expiration date by going to the airlines shopping portal and buying something cheap. Making a purchase on the shopping site qualifies for "activity" and miles expiration date is extended. Just a buy a $10 item that you'll need anyway. #flying

189. Do this after you buy a plane ticket

After purchasing a plane ticket, check back frequently for the next twenty-four hours. Most airlines will let you cancel with that time and if you find a lower fare, cancel the old fare and book the new one. #flying

190. Check this out if you have to sleep in an airport

Want to spend a night in an airport or perhaps you are forced to spend a night? Check out this site for tips. www.sleepinginairports.net. #flying

191. How to get around the return ticket issue

Many countries will not allow you to enter if you do not have a return flight ticket. You can buy a return ticket just before departure and then cancel it after arrival if you really don't know your return dates and times. Airlines allow 24 hours to cancel although flight aggregators like Orbitz, Expedia, etc., do not offer this same cancellation policy. Be sure to check first. #flying

192. Taxi fare tip

Taxi meters are only used in a few countries. Always negotiate the fare **before** you get in the cab when you're in countries that have taxis without meters. #taxi

193. Do this before leaving the rental car lot

When renting a car, before you drive off the rental car lot, use the video on your cell phone camera and walk slowly around the vehicle documenting any scratches or dents. #cars

194. How to get status on a second airline

If you have status with a certain hotel chain, rental car company or airline, call competitors and ask if they'll 'status match' you with their program. Many will do this quickly although you'll probably have to email a picture of your card or statement and they may ask for a couple of transactions within a few months to keep the status. #flying

195. Use this tip to get an upgrade at the hotel

Email the general manager of the hotel before you arrive. Let him/her know about your travel plans and be sure to mention anything special about your trip – such as anniversary, wedding, birthday, etc. You may be surprised

upon check-in when you're upgraded to a
nicer room. #hotel

196. Do this before leaving on vacation

Check daily deal sites such as Groupon.com
and LivingSocial.com for deals in the city you
plan to visit. You'll find hotels, restaurants,
and attractions at deep discounts. #general

197. Get a great rate on longer hotel stays

If you plan to stay at a hotel for a week or
longer, you should definitely call the hotel
direct and negotiate a better rate. Hotels
make more money when guests stay a long
time versus flipping the room every day.
Start out by asking for a 60% discount offer
their website rate for a daily room. You
might not get that deep discount but they
may counter-offer with something close to it.
#hotel

197. This tip will get you a hotel upgrade

Use the $20 tip at hotel check-in for an upgrade. Slip the $20 between your credit card and driver's license. Let the clerk know you're interested in an upgrade if available. In my experience, this works about 75% of the time. I've been upgraded to corner suites, fantasy suites, offered free parking, free buffets and more. In Hawaii, I booked the cheapest room. The $20 got me an oceanfront suite with a living room, bedroom, and double balcony! Visit www.frontdesktip.com for more information. #hotel

198. Google Maps tip

Download Google Maps to your smartphone. Enter destinations of places you'll visit and Google maps will put a star near them and make traveling easier. #general

199. Do you need a VISA?

Don't forget visas if traveling internationally. Many countries require a visa. If you don't have one when checking in at the airport, they'll send you home!

200. Do this when you don't speak the language

Learn a couple of useful phrases for countries you'll visit. At a minimum, learn 'Hello,' 'Thank you,' 'Where is the toilet?' and 'Please.' If you really want to make friends, learn to say, "you have beautiful eyes" or, "you have a beautiful smile." #general

201. Know this about your passport

Know the expiration date on your passport. Many recommend renewing with six months before expiration but I always renew with one year remaining. Some countries won't allow you to enter if your passport renews in six months or less. #general

202. Do this with your passport

Memorize – yes memorize – your passport number and expiration date. #general

203. Always check your passport for this

If you travel a lot, make sure you have blank pages for immigration stamps at the countries you'll be visiting. You may be denied entry if you don't have a blank stamp area in your passport! #general

204. Spread it around

Spread some of your money around. Put $100 in your checked bag and your laptop case. If you lose your wallet or are robbed, this backup money may come in handy. #general

205. Write reviews on TripAdvisor then do this

At hotel check-in, be sure to mention if you write reviews on Tripadvisor. You may get a nice upgrade. #hotel

206. Here's how to override the hotel thermostat

Many hotels control how cold – or hot – you can set the thermostat in your room. You can override this by changing to "VIP" mode. Watch this twelve-second video to see how to do it.

https://www.youtube.com/watch?v=H9zV4kO Vtg #hotel

207. Extra key for hotel room

Some hotels and cruise ships require you put your room key card into a slot by the door to activate air conditioning, heater, and lights. You can override this by asking the front desk for a second key and leaving it in the slot. Or, put an old membership card or credit card in the slot. A business card may even work. #hotel

208. Always drink this water in this city

The water is Rome Italy flowing from public drinking fountains is some of the purest in the world. Drink up! #general

209. Know the carry-on size limits

As of the date of this book, here are the carry-on size limits for U.S. airlines (in inches): 22x14x9 – American, Delta, United, US Airways and Hawaiian. 22x18x10 – Spirit. 24x16x10 – Frontier, Jet Blue, Southwest and Virgin America. 24x17x10 – Alaska. Size limits used to be generally ignored by airlines but they're clamping down now and may force you to check if oversized. #flying

210. Find out how long TSA lines are before you leave home

Download the "MyTSA" app to your phone. The app gives you real-time information on TSA security check-points at most airports in the U.S.A. #flying

211. Don't bring the whole bottle

Empty contact lens cases can be useful for makeup creams while traveling. #general

212. Pack jewelry like this

Place jewelry between two sheets of Glad Press n' Seal then put in your luggage. #luggage

213. Check and check again

Airlines change their prices during the day. Three changes a day are not unusual. Check back in a few hours if you don't like the prices shown. #flying

214. Do this to stop pickpockets

A paper clip will keep your zipper pulls together on your luggage and carry-on bag.

It will also prevent pickpockets from opening and stealing your valuables. #general

215. Jet lag cure

I know someone that swears he has the best cure for jet lag. Two days prior to departure, he gives up coffee. Upon landing, he has a double espresso. #flying

216. Take your old sneakers

Instead of tossing your old sneakers in the trash, save them for your next trip. Use them and then leave them in the trash on your way back home. You'll probably need the extra room on the way home. #general

217. Don't use this Wi-Fi

Never use a free Wi-Fi spot for banking or other sensitive transactions. #general

218. The hidden counter in the hotel room

Need extra counter space in a hotel room? Look in the closet for an ironing board. In a pinch, it can turn into a counter. #hotel

219. Nightlight in a hotel room

If you're used to a night light at home while sleeping, bring one on vacation and plug it in the wall socket in your hotel room. #hotel

220. Solo women traveler tip

Women traveling solo should be last to enter the elevator – and last to push the floor button also. #general

221. Wear shoes to the airplane toilet

If you're like me, you take off your shoes upon settling into your plane seat. My feet and socks are always clean so I don't think its offensive to those nearby, however. I ALWAYS put them on when going to the lavatory. Not because I'm ashamed to walk down the aisle with no shoes. Rather, it's because men have trouble hitting the toilet and the floor is, well, gross! #flying

222. See if your cruise ship offers unlimited Wi-Fi – before it's too late!

I am a heavy Wi-Fi user. I recently was on a Norwegian cruise for nine days around the Baltic sea. On day three of the cruise, I saw a flyer in my room that I had not read when I boarded. It said I could upgrade to unlimited Wi-Fi for the duration of the cruise for $25 per day. However, I had to sign-up for this plan by the end of day two on the cruise. I missed it! I ended up buying chunks of minutes and paid a lot more for Wi-Fi over the nine days plus, I had to quickly get on and off so I wouldn't use up my minutes. Lesson learned! #cruise

223. Check for hidden cameras in your hotel room or AirBnB room

Before I retired, one of the jobs I had was selling software to casinos in Las Vegas. A VP proudly told me they had about a dozen rooms where they had hid cameras behind pinholes. He said if they suspected cheaters, they would "upgrade" them to these rooms and then spy on them to see if they could learn more about their cheating. This was in 1997 and today, hidden cameras are everywhere. Do a search on Amazon for spy camera and you'll see over a thousand products. They are in clocks, remote controls, electrical plugs, smoke detectors, spray bottles, and much more. #hotels

224. Here's an easy tip for solving bad pillows in hotel rooms.

I hate soft, thin pillows. Sometimes, a hotel will only have these types on the bed. Remove the pillow from the pillowcase. Fold a couple of bath towels and stuff into the empty pillowcase. Many times, this is better for me than using the hotel pillows. #hotels

225. Try another gate agent when a flight is delayed.

I previously suggested you get on the phone immediately when you hear an announcement your flight has been canceled or seriously delayed. Another tip is to walk to another gate while you're on the phone. The agent at that gate is not required to help you but many times, you'll get the help you need. #flying

226. It might be more expensive to book three nights in a hotel instead of booking three individual nights.

This doesn't always work but surprisingly, it works often. Let's say you want to stay in a hotel on a Wednesday, Thursday and Friday night. If you book three separate reservations instead of one reservation for a three-night stay, it could actually be at a lower overall rate. #hotels

227. Wear sunscreen on the plane? Maybe

If you're sitting next to the window with the shade up, you should have sunscreen protecting your face. Those UV rays are powerful. Skin cancer is serious. #flying

228. Don't forget to clean the lens on your camera or phone camera.

I used to own a photo lab that printed images on canvas, slate, metal, cups, coasters, etc. Many times we were asked to clean-up an image that had smudges. These vacation photos had smudges because they forgot to clean the lens beforc taking pictures. Professional photographers are constantly cleaning lenses but if you rarely use your camera, you probably don't think about it. If you're like me, the lens on my camera phone gets smudged almost immediately in the morning. We usually forget this when we take those must-have vacation photos. A lens cleaning cloth is best for cleaning (the kind that came with your glasses) but in a pinch, your shirt will be better than nothing. Camera pros right now are groaning over me suggesting you use a shirt! #general

229. Control the hotel TV with your phone.

I don't like even touching remotes in hotel rooms let alone using them. Download the StayConnect app to your phone and you'll be able to control the hotel TV from your phone. Change channels. Control volume. It doesn't work with all hotel TV's but it works with many of them. #hotels

230. How to avoid having lost luggage returned to your home instead of your hotel.

If you're travelling to a hotel for an extended visit, put the address of the hotel on your bag tags, not your home address. If your bags are lost, you'll want them at your hotel, not back home. #general

231. Always carry id in Europe.

You may not know this but it's the law in many European countries. You must have a valid id at all times. I know I've broken this law many times but I won't do it again. #general

232. Use a battery operated candle in your cruise cabin.

Cruise lines won't allow open fires in your cabin but you can use a battery operated candle. Add a little ambiance to your cabin along with having a night light. #cruise

233. Get your money if bumped.

If you're denied boarding because the plane is full and you have a valid reservation, airlines are required to pay you 200% of the cost of you ticket. That amount doubles if the airlines can't get you to your final destination within two hours of scheduled arrival time. Don't let the airlines try to give you less. #flying

234. Use the WiFox app to get passwords for every airport lounge around the world.

Download this handy app to your phone. It's continually updated from users with passwords at private lounges at airports around the world. #flying

235. Book cruise excursions even if you're not sure you'll want them later.

Popular excursions fill up fast on cruise ships. Go ahead and book them because most cruise lines allow you to cancel later without a penalty.

Of course, be sure your cruise line allows cancellations. #cruise

236. Join mail lists for all airlines you may want to fly. You'll get limited time offers for huge savings.

Today, I received an email from Hawaiian Air announcing a two-day sale on roundtrip tickets from California to Hawaii. This was a super sale and it was only for forty-eight hours. If I wasn't a member of their mail list, I would not have known about this sale. #general

237. Use cashback sites like Ebates.

I'm not paid or sponsored by Ebates and I'll get nothing for recommending them, however you should use this site when booking flights, hotels, cruises, etc. You'll get up to 10% cash back. Last month, they sent me $110 just for purchases I had made on various sites over the past few months. #general

238. Check both Uber and Lyft for best rates.

I was recently staying near Newark airport and used Uber and Lyft twice a day for a week. I checked each service before requesting a car. The rates were never the same and while one was cheaper at certain times, the other would be cheaper at certain times. Have both apps on your phone. #cars

239. Don't carry a lot of cash.

Your chance of being robbed is higher when you travel. As much as we try, we stand-out from locals and look like tourists. Tourists are more likely to be robbed. #general

240. If you are checking bags, bring an extra outfit on your carry-on

Once I was on a ten-day cruise and met a couple on day one that had their bags delayed from the flight. On day two, they were wearing a cruise ship sweatshirt purchased in the gift shop. They wore the same shirt on day three. On day four, they wore a new shirt again purchased on the cruise ship. Finally, their bags caught up with the ship. Because of this, if I must check bags, and I try very hard not to check, I make sure I have back up clothes in my carryon. #general

241. Download maps to restaurants and sites to your phone before leaving home.

When traveling, always download directions for cities you'll be visiting to your phone. They are handy and you won't have to worry about finding Wi-Fi to download them when you need them. #general

242. Pack meals

Restaurants can be very expensive in tourist areas. Why not put some instant oatmeal pouches in your luggage and then just add hot water? These make a very cheap breakfast right in your hotel room. #hotels

243. Get a free layover in a foreign city.

When traveling abroad, it is usually easy to book a flight where the layover is 15-20 hours. Let's say you're traveling from Los Angeles to Israel. You can probably get a long layover in Amsterdam or London. #flying

244. Alcohol at altitude is worse on your body than alcohol on the ground.

High altitude thins your blood and alcohol is absorbed differently. Two drinks is probably equivalent to three or four on the ground. #flying

245. Don't use airline headphones.

Those earbuds passed out free by flight crews may not be sanitary. It's a well-known fact, they are many times not cleaned and just put back in a bag and sealed. They may look new and fresh but may be dirty. #flying

246. Don't buy products from airline catalogs

Those catalogs in the seatback in front of you are ridiculously expensive and over-priced. You can find every item online for sometimes 50% less than the airline catalog price. #flying

247. Tip the flight crew

Flight crews are usually overworked and underpaid. They don't start getting paid until the door of the plane closes and may have to buy their own meals. Plus, they have to always be pleasant while dealing with problem passengers. When you buy that drink, slip them a couple bucks. Or, give them a small gift like the one I use which is a lapel pin of a plane with an angel on the wing. #flying

248. Best flight fares are usually on Tuesday

Flights are usually more expensive on Mondays and Fridays and often have the lowest prices on Wednesdays. #flying

249. The day of boarding usually has great offers for spas, restaurants, tours, etc.

When you board a cruise, don't just walk by the crew soliciting offers. Some are very good and most are only offered on day one of the cruise. #cruise

250. Never disobey flight crews

The pilot has the same authority as a ship captain. You can be arrested and even bound to your seat if you disobey a flight crew member. On the flip side, the captain can perform marriages to passengers. #flying

251. Take a hotel bus then catch Uber or Lyft

At some airports, Uber and Lyft are not allowed to pick-up passengers. Just take the first hotel bus that comes along, tip the driver and buck, and get off at the hotel. While on the bus, order your ride and it will be waiting for you at the hotel. #flying

252. Fill up your rental car with gas

If you don't return your rental with a full tank, the rental agency will charge around 140% more than the gas station you passed on your way to the airport. #flying #cars

253. Print your boarding pass at home AND at the airport

If you're late arriving at the gate, the airlines can close the door early and leave even if you printed your boarding pass at home. If you print again when you arrive at the airport, their computer will know you're at the airport and they'll leave on-time. #flying

254. Use your carryon as a footrest when you have a bulkhead seat.

You must put your carryon in the overhead bin for takeoff and landing but there is no rule against putting it in front of you and propping your feet on it. #flying

255. A plunger on a train

This may take the prize for the craziest tip on this list but use a mini-plunger stuck to the ceiling of a tram at the airport as a handrail. Of course, you'll have to carry the mini-plunger in your carryon but that's another story. #general

256. Another reason to rent cars from CostcoTravel

I love CostcoTravel.com and always rent my cars from that site. Usually, their rates are much lower than other places. I'm not paid to say that either. One of their benefits is additional drivers added to the rental are at zero cost. #cars

257. Don't carry your hotel key in the sleeve with your room number

If your purse is stolen, the thief will know your hotel and room number plus, they'll have a key to your room. Text the room number to your phone, or take a picture, then leave the sleeve in your room. #hotel

258. How to keep the center seat empty on a Southwest Airlines flight

Here's one I won't ever do but it's up to you. Wear a surgical mask and put a box of tissue on your lap. Everybody will walk right by that empty seat. #flying

259. Earn points instead of having your room cleaned

I told you in another tip I don't like having housekeepers in my room while I'm away. Many hotel chains will reward you with frequent reward points if you decline room cleaning at check-in. You can still order fresh towels and other items but you'll be padding your account by skipping the bed-making and trash emptying. #hotel

260. Ask Siri "What plane is overhead?"

If you have an iPhone, this will work. Try it! #flying

Printed in Great Britain
by Amazon